I0003979

DELETE BOOKS ON

KINDLE DEVICES.

A 100% GUIDE ON HOW TO
REMOVE BOOKS FROM ALL
YOUR KINDLE DEVICES IN 1
MINUTES.

JAMEY CRANE

© 2019 JAMEY CRANE

This publication may not be reproduced, distributed or transmitted by any means without the prior written consent of the author first had and obtained. The information offered here is for the purposes of information only and is universal as such. The information presented here is without any form of contract or guarantee or indemnity whether with the reader or any third party.

TABLE OF CONTENTS

BOOKS TO DELETE

Deleting books from your Kindle device, App on iPad & iPhone, or cloud, is very easy although it is not as straightforward as we like it to be. Also note that if you want to permanently delete books from your Kindle or Kindle Cloud is possible but it is not obvious; I believe this because Amazon does not want you to mistakenly delete a book that you have already paid leading to a repurchase. Majorly at times, when people want to delete a book from their Kindle, what they really want to do is remove it from the Kindle app on iPhone or iPad or to delete the book from their Kindle device and will want to keep the e-book in the Kindle Cloud, since they paid for it. There are several ways to delete or remove Kindle books and a handful places from which you might want to remove or delete these books. In this book, we shall be covering how to delete books from Kindle devices, as well as how to remove books from the Kindle app on iPhone or iPad. It does not really matter the model of Kindle that you owned, deleting books is very similar.

HOW DELETE BOOKS ON KINDLE DEVICE USING PC

1. Connect kindle to computer

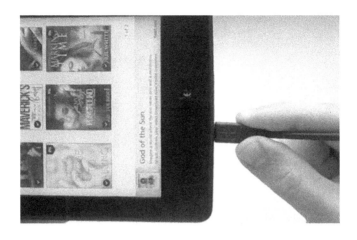

2. Lunch Kindlian

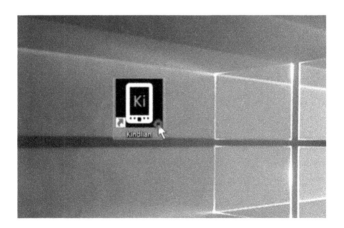

3. Scan your Device and transfer books to PC

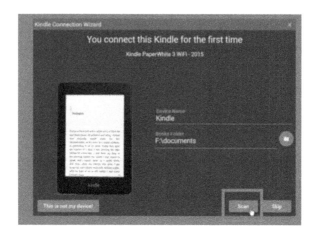

4. Select Kindle in the left column and remove all books

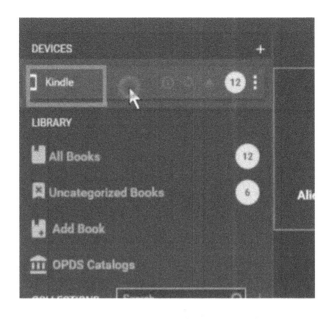

5. Click on remove books from
   Device

6. Open PC Library and copy needed books back to kindle

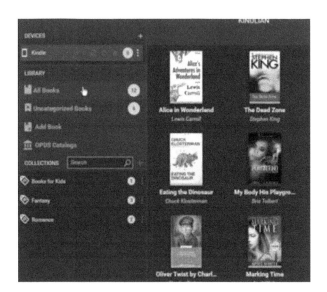

7. Now your device is clean

HOW TO DELETE BOOKS ON IPHONE & IPAD KINDLE APP

You have a Library in the Kindle app containing all of your books. You can delete PDFs and book samples that you may have downloaded to your device, but as for e-books that you purchased, they are stored in your Kindle Cloud and they cannot be deleted within the app or on Kindle devices except on Amazon website. These books that you purchased although cannot be deleted permanently using your Kindle Devices or App, they can however, be archived, this is to say that the book is removed from the Kindle app on your iPad or iPhone but it still however remains in your Cloud and is available to be re-downloaded whenever you choose to. To remove or delete a book from your Kindle app on your iPad or iPhone use the follow steps:

Step 1

Open the Kindle app on your iPhone or iPad.

Step 2

Navigate to your Library. You can do this by clicking on the icon in the top left corner of the screen.

Step 3

Tap either Library or All Items.

Step 4

Select Device at the bottom. You will be seeing only your books downloaded to your iPad or iPhone. All these books you are able to access and read even when you are offline.

At the bottom left corner is an icon that allows you switch between your items in grid mode and list mode.

Step 5

Tap and hold the book to see your options such as Delete Permanently or Remove from Device (for purchased books) if you are viewing your items in grid mode. Or

If you are viewing your items using the list mode, delete or archive a book a sample by swiping left and click on either Delete or Archive.

Please note that books archived or removed from your device will still be found in your Kindle Cloud except you go to manage your device to delete them completely.

HOW TO DELETE BOOKS ON KINDLE E-READER

Kindles E-Reader are great device that can store hundreds of books in one place. There may however, come a time when you need to delete some of these books from your collection, either as a result of space or simply because you don't want the book anymore. There are two basic ways in which you can delete books from your Kindle E-reader. The first one can be done right on your device by navigating to the book you no longer want and select it to "remove from device" while on the second note, you can permanently delete the book through your Kindle account on your web browser.

Step 1

On your E-Reader Home Screen navigate through your library until you locate the book you want to delete and select it.

Step 2

Select "Remove from Device." Once the book is deleted or remove from your device, it will go into your Archive.

OR

Step 3

To delete a book permanently, you have to sign into your Amazon account

Step 4

Select "Manage Your Content and Devices." Locate the book you want to delete and tick the small box on the left side of the title.

Step 5

Select "delete." You will be prompted to confirm whether or not you want to delete the file.

Step 6

Click "Yes" to confirm that you want to remove the file from your library.

HOW TO DELETE BOOKS ON KINDLE KEYBOARD

In deleting books from your kindle, you must understand that your kindle has a 5-way directional controller. This are the keys we will be using to delete your unwanted books

Step 1

The first step is to press your home key and navigate to the book you want to delete.

Step 2

Navigate to the name of the book from your Kindle Library or Home screen, and then press the Left toggle on the 5-way controller.

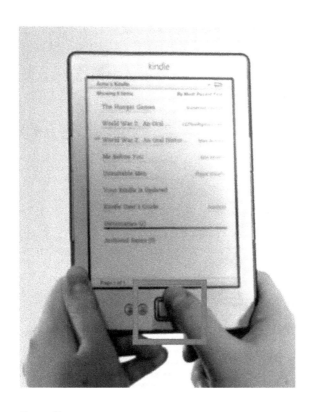

Step 3

Select Remove or delete from Device.

Press the center of the 5-way controller.

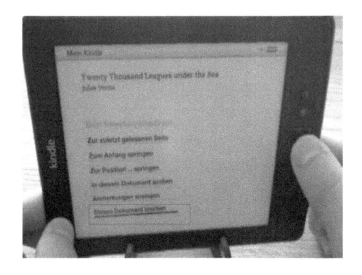

Please pardon my device language, just
follow the steps as directed here and you
will get the same result that you desire.

Step 4

A menu will pop up asking you if you
desire to delete the book. Hit on the okay
button at the bottom of your device to
have the book deleted or removed.

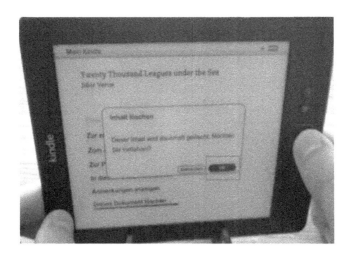

Please be aware that this will only remove the book from your Kindle device and has not permanently delete the book.

If you want to go one step further to delete the book permanently, Log onto your Amazon web site and click on Manage your Kindle

Go further to the action button at the right hand side of your device and click on it for a drop down menu and "Locate Delete from library"

Confirm that that you want to delete it by clicking on <u>Yes</u> on the pop up Menu to finally delete your book. From this step, note that it is only books that you don't want again that you should delete because once the books are deleted from here, they cannot be recovered again.

HOW TO REMOVE BOOKS ON HD FIRE

At the top of your device, go to where it says books

Make sure your device is on Orange colour because if you are on cloud, you will tend to see more books because cloud will show you all the books you have ever bought.

Hold down on the book and a
notification will pop up asking you to
either add to favorite or remove from
device.

Click on remove from device and the
book will be deleted.

HOW TO PERMANENTLY DELETE BOOKS FROM KINDLE CLOUD

The storage for your Kindle books in the Amazon Cloud is unlimited. Kindle Cloud can contain as many wonderful novels as you may like and never run out of space for keeping them. You can

however, you can choose to permanently delete books from your account for reasons best known to you. It is important to reemphasize that books deleted from your cloud are gone and you can't access them unless you repurchase them. So therefore before you delete books from the Kindle Cloud on your iPad, iPhone, or Kindle device you should have a rethink. To permanently delete a book from cloud, you will have to log in to your Amazon account in a web browser. Use the following step to permanently delete books from your Amazon Kindle Library and your Kindle Cloud:

Step 1

Log in to your Amazon account on your
in a web browser.

Step 2

Move your mouse over Account & Lists
at the top of your computer and this will
bring a drop down menu.

Step 3

Select Manage Your Content and
Devices from the drop down menu.

Step 4

Find the book(s) you want to delete your
devices.

Step 5

Click to check the box to the left of the title you want to remove.

Step 6

Click Delete near the top.

Manage Your Content and Devices

Your Content

| Show | Books ÷ | All ÷ | Sort By | Purchase Date Newest-Oldest ÷ |

| Deliver (1) | Delete (1) | Deselect All |

Select Actions Title

Your First 1000 Copies: The Step-by-Step Guide to Marketing kindleunlimited

KLOUT SCORE: Social Media Influence: How to Gain Exposure kindleunlimited

250 Things You Should Know About Writing

Step 7

Confirm, "Yes, delete permanently."

HOW TO DELETE BOOKS ON PAPERWHITE

To delete books from your kindle Paperwhite device is no way different from any other Kindle device. To delete, use the following steps.

Step 1

Log in to your Amazon account on your in a web browser.

Step 2

Move your mouse over Account & Lists at the top of your computer and this will bring a drop down menu.

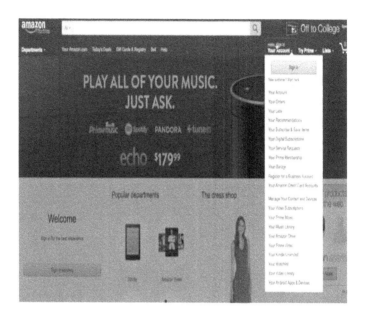

Step 3

Select Manage Your Content and
Devices from the drop down menu.

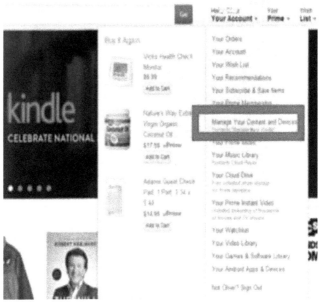

Step 4

Find the book(s) you want to delete your devices.

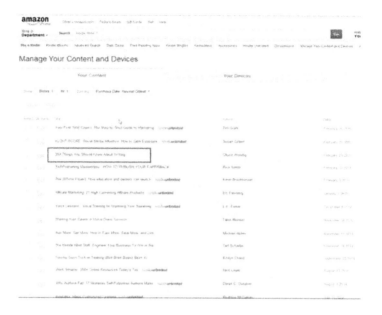

Step 5

Click to check the box to the left of the title you want to remove.

	The 20Time Project: How educators and parents can launch kindleunlimited	Kevin Brookhouser
	Affiliate Marketing: 27 High Converting Affiliate Products kindleunlimited	Ely Feinberg
	Voice Lessons : Vocal Training for Improving Your Speaking kindleunlimited	L. K. Fisher
	Starting Your Career in Voice-Overs (Sample)	Talon Beeson
	Ask More, Get More: How to Earn More, Save More, and Live	Michael Alden
	The Mobile Mind Shift: Engineer Your Business To Win in the	Ted Schadler
	Tommy Goes Trick-or-Treating (Bird Brain Books Book 4)	Emilye Chand
	Work Smarter: 350+ Online Resources Today's Top kindleunlimited	Nick Loper
	Why Authors Fail: 17 Mistakes Self-Published Authors Make kindleunlimited	Derek C. Doepker
	Inevitable: Mass Customized Learning kindleunlimited	Beatrice McGarvey
	Creative Workshop: 80 Challenges to Sharpen Your Design kindleunlimited	David Sherwin

Step 6

Click Delete near the top.

Step 7

Confirm, "Yes, delete permanently."

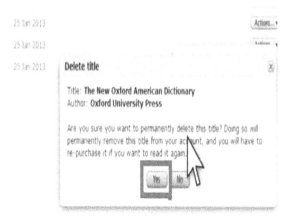

HOW TO DELETE BOOKS ON KINDLE APP FOR ANDROID

To delete books from your kindle android device is no way different. At the bottom right corner of every books you downloaded, there is a checkmark. To delete, use the following steps

Step 1

Hold down the checkmark to select the book. Once the book is checked, you can touch other titles that you want to delete as well to check them.

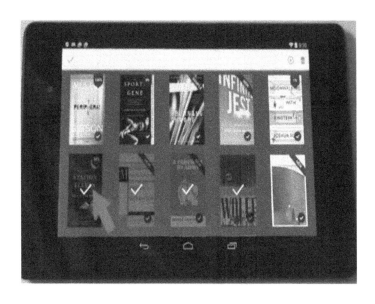

Step 2

At the right top corner of the screen, you
will discover that there is a thrash icon,
and by tapping on the thrash icon, it
removes those books that you have check
marked.

www.ingramcontent.com/pod-product-compliance
Lightning Source LLC
LaVergne TN
LVHW041221050326
832903LV00021B/735